Praise for

Sana Sana

Delias's poetry offers sharp and indelible apertures into the complicated beauty of a world she has lived intimately. It is an emotional and human world that is grounded in the rich and gritty geography of South Texas, and Delias welcomes us with clarity and grace.

—**Michael Saenger**, Professor of English
at Southwestern University, author of
Shakespeare and the French Borders of English

Sana Sana

FLOWERSONG
PRESS

poetry by

Ashlynn Delias

FLOWERSONG
P R E S S

FlowerSong Press
Copyright © 2025 by Ashlynn Delias
ISBN: 978-1-963245-85-1

Published by FlowerSong Press
in the United States of America.
www.flowersongpress.com

Set in Adobe Garamond Pro

NOTICE: SCHOOLS AND BUSINESSES
FlowerSong Press offers copies of this book at quantity discount with
bulk purchase for educational, business, or sales promotional use. For
information, please email the Publisher at info@flowersongpress.com.

DEDICATED TO

My parents
For making me
Me

Chicana
Funny
Yet
Poetic
And deep

AND TO MY PROFESSOR

Dr. Sonia Del Hierro

For showing me
That I don't have to pick a single narrative

For nurturing a world
Where Latina gringas like me
Can proudly be
Both.

table of contents

McAllen

Six Hours North

Detour

Sana Sana

McAllen

The identity that lives in the river

I am Chicana
I am white-skinned
With a big, Mexican nose
I'm not *real* Latina
With swinging hips and a voluptuous chest
With bronze skin and dark tresses–of hair
I am not the blonde *guerita* all the *morenitos* pine after
My eyes aren't blue–they are mucky brown–the color of the Rio
Grande River
That all the *mojados* cross over
My Spanglish is as broken as the border between Weslaco, Tejas
and Tamaulipas, Mexico
My Latina roots shove through my white skin
Like the desperate manos flailing between the concrete walls of
the border tunnel
Hoping some naive *gringa* will pull them through into their
American dream
Where brown skin gleams white and black eyes glint green
Where *flacas* buy their boobs and butts in a building
While Mexicanas get called sluts for theirs
Where curly hair only counts if you permed it
And kinky hair is "done" by being stick straightened
Where Latina parts are best stuck on a white body
You can't live in the middle
You can't straddle between

In between is where you'll find me
I guess my ancestors dropped me off

On their way from Guanajuato
Right before they crossed
To good ol' Texan country
And so they made me who I am
Existing in the middle
Of America and the Motherland

Make America Great Again

Sana Sana colita de rana
Can this song work to heal generational trauma?

Si no sanas hoy
 sanaras mañana

Turn men back to boys
'fore they were stripped from their mamas?

Sana sana colita de rana
They played on their way
To Tijuana

Si no sanas hoy
Sanaras mañana

Make America Great Again
I just lost my mama.

Roots

Michigan cotton
White in burning skies
Scarecrow lines on sunburnt faces
Backs that brace with leather-whip bidden pain
And hunch over all the same– with laughter:

I was raised by those who see the sunshine
In every fatal natural disaster.

Consummation–I mean–colonization

A meadow on the horizon
Peace
Closer, come closer
Scant purple flowers
Warm lilting air
Peace perfect
Come, closer
Walking
No, running
Flowers grow larger
Hazy purple into
Brilliant blue
Running
Sweating
Climbing
I see it
Jagged
Rocks
Seemed
closer in the distance
Easier
Bolder
Lots of them
Bleeding hands
Climb
Climb faster
Throw your legs over
The ledge

The meadow
Thicket
Enveloping me
I become soil
Fertilizing her roots
With my blood
She is
my own–

Red
Creeping grass
Shrinking
Into
Crowns of thorns
Stinging
Precious petals
With Consummation
Her pollen becomes
My blood
Happy Thanksgiving.

My mom is always telling me to dye my hair blonde

She means well
(That's what I tell myself)
Commenting that my hair needs
some "ummf"
And she's right–right?
She means well
I
Was less than 9
When I found out
That beauty means
Turning every brown thing
My grandpa picked in fields
Into cotton white.

My dad worked for *la migra*

He's the kindest man I've ever known
Never discriminating an individual based on how they cast their
vote
He is more compassionate than most
La migra–but more tolerant than my neighbors
Who proudly plant a Trump flag on their lawn
La migra-yet contempts the very pole that controversy stands
upon
He doesn't stand for that kind of character
He is a friend to all
But because of his job
I
Am a friend
To   none.

My dad worked for *la migra* pt 2

I'll forever be doomed to sit outside the fence
Of all my Mexican friends
Because of what my dad does

So I play pretend
That my mother's family
Didn't come from Guanajuato
That she raised me like a full-bred alma de casa
She makes enchiladas–
We walk to Progreso on the weekends.

Eventually

Today I
Spoke full Spanish to the waiter
And felt proud
I used to think
I'd have to lock myself in a room,
Throw away the key
Devote my life to learning
Yet we are always–
Becoming–

Life is a process
Why force its hand?
If it's in you, it will come
A geiser bubbling up
Eventually.

Karma never came

Or he did
And he keeps getting the wrong person
Why else would the *morenitos* keep dying?

Karma is a bitch
So he's a girl–
By definition

I don't think so
Because women always finish
The job correctly–
Karma hasn't.

Wisdom

I think you can tell a lot about a person
By the way they deal with animals:
My grandma tolerates them
Allows them at her house
Warns, "they better not go to the bathroom
in here,"

But my grandpa
Has an ease about him
Laughs when my dog's fur floats in the air
He doesn't try to control mess
He accepts that its there
I don't even think that he distinguishes "mess"
He just accepts things
For what they are.

Scarecrow lines

Are what I see
When I picture
My grandfather in my head

I hope to leave a mark
As deep as he left his
In the corners of our eyes
In the widening of our smiles.

Vick's

Vicks in our socks
Under all our clothes
Hell, my mom even made me swallow it
When I had a sore throat.

It's too bad
That vicks couldn't heal
A marriage some phase past dead—

Many in this barrio have failed to break this cycle
So we just sleep
On a half-empty bed
With vicks on our chest.

Immigrant

I asked my grandfather
About his days as a cherry-picker
Expecting to hear horror stories–
Bloody knuckles and white men–
Yet when he looked back
All he could do was smile and laugh

That's not because
His life wasn't hard–it was
Full of pain, but that's the kind of man my granddad is
He focuses on the good in everything.

So many lost tales in this town

I've had things in my head
And not the strength to write them down
Stories become
A sad glance in an eye
That was once fleeting
Now passed down
Generation to generation
Becoming a whole city
The most powerful stories
Are these–that speak in silence
Through dull child eyes
A quick peek
Pages and pages
With no spine to bind.

Don't marry a Mexican

Mi mama siempre me decía
They're stubborn
machismo
wife beaters
They'll pay your bills–
Only to cheat on you

Mi mama siempre me decía
This may be true
Pero,
¿Quién los va a arreglar?

¿Who will heal our land?

This whole town's the barrio
Everybody's been here
Since
Nobody can remember when
So-and-so went to jail
So-and-so is dead

An unending cycle
The salvaged are the ones who fled
Who will stay and heal this barrio?
That only *las manos de Dios*
Could mend.

Grandpa

My granddad isn't a grave man
He laughs with ease
Feeds the dogs with his hands
When you look into his eyes
They've lived a lot of life.

Sad eyes

Is what he used to call me
I had a cloud over my head
He was the only one who could see it
Or maybe just, the only one
Who never
Ignored it.

Everything is done better by whites

Tan is good if it comes from a spray can
Bad if it comes from back-breaking work in the heat

Curls are good if they come from a chemical bottle
Bad if they are frizzy, thick, and poof in Caribbean humidity

Curves are good if you bought them from a white man with a
Harvard degree
Bad if they are from beans and rice–natural handles gathering

White girls' artificiality is praised
Latina beauty is criticized, envied, and shamed
Stolen by barbies who think they can do *india, gordita, y morenita*
better than we can
Nothing's better than brown taken, reclaimed, and deformed in
white privileged hands.

Medicine can only do so much

Vicks on my feet
Cozied by my socks
Vicks on my chest
Will I put Vicks on my heart?
When there's nothing left.

Sunday morning

I'm wearing leggings to church today,

The foofy mothers will say,
You came to God's house like *that?*

The Pentecostals down the street will ask them–
In all their pink-cheeked huffiness–
Why they feel the need to wear makeup before God
What are you trying to hide?

Sins, old age
The fact that there's people who don't know the love of God
And we're *inside*
Fighting about lipstick.

Una Latina Gringa

I'll let my Spanish grow
With my hair and nails
Cut it
Trim it
Here and there
My roommate will say, " damn your hair got so long,"
I'll speak a whole conversation
Realizing,
I've been fluent for some time.

In the summers, I work at a restaurant

Everyone in the kitchen speaks Spanish
They call me "guera"
"Gringa"
Both those things mean *beautiful*
My skin is lighter than all the kitchen staff
My hair is the color of chestnuts instead of coal
I feel slimy
Because here where nearly everyone comes from Mexico
White is still beautiful–
Brown, a burden to those who wear her.

Divorce

This happens
To so many like me
Who felt unseen
As the adults they had to be in their homes—
Young flowers
Barely blooming
But already wilted.

Here comes the bride

I went to a white elephant
My cousin's new boyfriend came
It was the first time her mom met *Antoni*
You'd think the very vowels of his name stunk
By the pain in her face

She interrogated him
Telling him point-blank
"When she gets married, I'm only buying the wedding dress,"
"It's a Mexican tradition," my mom says–
"To have the guy pay for the whole thing."

I hope whoever I marry understands Mexicans–
I'm afraid.

Love me, love me not

He loves me
I'm a petal in the wind
He loves me not
A fragment— an echo—a bloom that once was
He loves me
I'm as light as air
He loves me not
I'm painfully aware that
He loves me
Petals wilt
He loves me not
The sun dies
He says,
that he loves me.

5 years I can barely remember and can't seem to forget

I should have known *you* were not
'the *one*'
 when I was pro-con listing you with my 15-year-old best friend
If
Not
Then
I should have known when
I felt insurmountable hesitation–
You asked me to be your girlfriend
I had to *think*
Mull you over
I chewed you up
Spit you out
And yet–
I said
Yes
To the idea of you
Although even the notion tasted terrible
If not
Even *then*
I should have known when
you said
–chill–
 laugh less
"You're causing a scene"
I guess

My main character energy
Reminded you
You were just the supporting actor
If
Not
Then
I should've known when
You lied to my face about your addiction to ecstasy
Seriously
A powder–your first mistress
Let's not forget
You were also a cheat
I should've known then–when
You said she was my IOS Upgrade
Or what about when
You said you'd rape me
"it's not a sin for *you* then"–criminal logic
Did I know then?
No–not even when
You made good on your threats
But never your promises
No, not even then
I wish I'd known when
I was 14–
with undiagnosed OCD
You saw the weakness
And like all good predators
You preyed on me

But next time, you write an 11-paged letter calling me "demon-possessed"
Don't you dare pray for me.

I am my mother's daughter

You shouted, "You're just like your mom,"
It was supposed to insult me–
Justify your adultery
I was stunned
I laugh, looking back

I am
Just like my mom

I've dealt with betrayal
After betrayal
And still my faith
Does not betray me

I bless those who curse me
Serve those who spit in my face

I am just like my mom
You called it conditional love
Yet love
Finds no joy
In unrighteousness

I always choose the right thing
Even if it comes as an apology

I'm just like my mom
The words used to feel like a horrific prophecy
6 years later–
I see the way
You complimented me.

Six Hours North

When I moved to college

My roommates told me I had an accent
Told me they could tell I was *something*
But not sure *what*
Just by seeing my Instagram pictures
That's when I learned:
Minorities are *things*
Not *whos*

Don't ever date someone who ate glue as a kid

I was only
Half of what you wanted
I gave
My whole self
To you

You called me shallow–
Ugly, too-serious
Biding my time on boring things–politics and religion–
Then I wasn't shallow like a pretty sitting trinket
I was hollow
Half-full, mostly empty

I thought I was–
Whole
You couldn't see that–
Gazing at me
Through the hole
That was in you

If I am filling
The hole
In you
I am only enough
To make you satisfied
With yourself–

And no one
Is satisfied
With only themselves—

I could not
Be me
And fix
You.

That is why
I thought I was,

Empty.

                              Inadequate.

Insufficient.

I could not
Be enough
For myself,
While using all my strength
To make

You

              Enough

For yourself

Your mistake
Was using me
As glue,

My mistake
Was believing
That glue
Was all I was destined to **be,**

I am not glue.
                    Stucco cracking–

In a fake mansion

I cannot–
Fill your holes
Without–
Becoming
A hole,
Myself–

I could only be
My whole self,
When I lost
The half,
That was
you.

What I know now

My fingers gripped the steering wheel with cold sweat.
 I could feel my heart beating in my throat, threatening to
explode out of my mouth in currents of dread.
I tried to listen to worship music–anything to drown out the
turmoil in my head.
That was the night you ghosted me out of our relationship–*how
21st century of you.*

And the sun rose to shine upon my harried doe eyes and
pound upon the place in my forehead that I was convinced
was wrinkling by the second due to the racing, cycling, endless,
worrisome thoughts in my head.
The fluffy tufts from the saucer chair in the corner of my room
cradled me–a shepherd cradling an anxious sheep to his chest.
My stomach flipped with the surreal truth, and my fingers shook
against the soft, still, secure, safe fuzz of the chair.
For once, my cloudy head was clear.
In the middle of the grey, black, knotted tangle of thoughts and
fears in my stomach
 was a faint light that seemed to engulf me until reality was wrung
from anxiety
 and faith collided with fear.
The wire that runs from my heart to my head that had failed
to connect over the years–the broken wire that drove me to
endure bruises, glass, abandoned houses, and missed calls–the
disconnected wire that made me believe I was

worthless,
        inadequate,
                voiceless,
                        and small–

had finally clicked into place as I felt the world around me fall.

I
        am
                loved.
And that's what I didn't know–

                        All those years ago–

When I thought I couldn't go on without you and took to
alcohol– and to terrible men that somehow couldn't reach your
standard of low. But

                                What

                                                I

know
 Now

Is that I can stand tall. And as I walk to the gentle voice that
calls–me "child." the voices of those who called me insufficient,
                        shameful,

                                stained,

                                        And

                replaceable

                        Stall.

Unraveling

People unravel
Like yarn
You don't fall apart
You merely see
What's been inside you,
All along.
Before life tangled you–bound you up–knotted you
With heartache
Pain
forgotten—truths–
Webs of lies–
Truth
Peace
Love
hides
Invisible between snarls and twists
You must become undone to truly exist.

Thoughts I think while driving but shouldn't

I could swerve
Let go
Of the steering wheel
Into oncoming traffic

I used to scare myself–
Not anymore
Death is an ease reaching out to me
We mourn the lost too presently
For me to paint another tragedy.

I had a conversation with my professor

She said the Chicanas would tell the postmodernists to "fuck off,"
So F–off
If your universal truth is so polite, it can be passed around like
carrots and hummus on a paper plate, in between a circle of
sheltered inheritance kids and courteously declined by those who
find it's flavor *slightly* disagreeable to their sensitive digestion
Then that wasn't a hard-fought truth–
You got into the history books for free—no one tried to write all
over you.

I go to a Liberal Arts University

My campus is held in the glove of a misty hand
The kind of fog that lingers on clothing like an insecure child
Clinging to his mother's leg
It seeps through the buttons of my jacket and creeps its way up
through my baggy jeans
The kind of mist that penetrates everything–

You can never stay warm or dry despite bundles and layers
It seeps and seeps until it's clinging tautly around your wrists
And turning every bone stone cold like the stare
Of all the sallow, defeated faces here

Did the weather deplete young students of their youthful vigor
Or did we suck all the blue out of the humid air?

My friend fell asleep on the side of the road

Stars fill the sky
I lean back in the passenger seat
I haven't seen this many stars in a long time

Its 4:00 am
You've slept too long
You never even set the alarm

I'm too afraid to wake you
I roll my head back until it touches my neck
I don't know when I'll see a sky like this next

When you move from the country to the city
You get used to the night sky looking like a cardboard box–
A lamp that someone threw a sheet over
A sky blazing with glitter comes as a shock

I hadn't realized that I hadn't seen stars
In so long.
I'd gotten used to the snowglobe–used to being numb

How did I settle into a world without stars–
Without noticing?
How did I fold the world into a jar
And call it exploring?

Dear perfectionist,

Roses bloom
For 6-8 weeks
Out of 52 — a year
Why do you
Punish yourself
For not blooming
Every
Single
 season?
This goes against nature's reason
In harsh winter
Roses appear
As sticks
Or hips
Alive, flourishing, yet dormant
You don't have to perform—
pretty pink petals
Every single moment
Flourishing looks like leafless stems
The way it looks like a bouquet in a lover's hands
You don't have to be the peak
Version of yourself
Every season
Blooms require rain and sun—
Dormant times let your roots deepen.

On my way to class

I'm running late–again.
I haven't been able to keep the nightmares out of my head.
In class, I feel like people can see the rain cloud hovering over
me– a rejected prom queen's crown.
Only the air around *me* is sticky.
I inhabit my own personal bubble of inclement weather,
Funny, I've always been known for my sunny disposition.

Poems you write when you are heartbroken at a wedding

Everyone is sobbing for the bride,
So am I,

That's halfway true
She walks down the aisle
He cries at the sight of her

How rare, how magical–love is a gift
One-in-a-million, forged by God's hand

She walks down the aisle
So do I
But I walk the other way
I leave you at the altar
of what will never be our wedding day.

Tears stream down all the women's painted cheeks
Tears stream down mine
Tears of joy–the fusing of two lives
It's also the ripping apart,
I cry
We come apart as they embark on a new life.

Pumpkin patch

This is the second year in a row
I've gone to the pumpkin patch with my friends

We hold a sign that says "you're the pumpkin to my spice"
I wish it was you
I wish I were here with someone who loved me

I am
Here
with someone who loves me

I
wouldn't trade these moments for anything.

Fall came around again

It's been a year
Since I wrote
The above
Teenage angst-y
Heart-wrenched angry poem
I went to a pumpkin patch
With a guy
For the first time
In three whole years
Leaves turn brown
Fall
And grow again
Time flies by
Hearts break
Then mend
Grains of sand
In an hourglass
One by one
Painful trickling
And then all at once
the time is gone.

Crying at a birthday party

Wow
I couldn't be more cliche
All dolled up in bright pink
Giving off a deep dark blue
You don't even miss me
Do you?

Fairy Tales

I became an adult when
I realized
That problems don't vanish,
At the strike of twelve,
Like my Fairy Godmother said.

I became an adult when
I realized
There's no glass slipper to leave behind,
No Prince Charming on his way to avenge
Erase
Redeem
Restore
My fairy tale's end.

I became an adult when
I realized
There's no magic wand to wave
To make betrayal go away
No genie's lamp to rub
To take away physical pain.

I became an adult when
I realized
There's no true love's kiss
Only kisses goodbye

No enchanted carpet
Or pumpkin to ride–
Away–
Into a dreamt-up paradise.

I am an adult and
I realize
That fairy tales are the hopes, of a pining person's head
We may not have green pixies to fly us to Neverland

Yet we are not left–without magic–
Instead we have legs
That ache but keep going
Hands that tremble, but keep holding–
Onto God's promises and word–
There are eyes that are blurred,
Yet filled with God's vision,
There are promises, that when believed, make castles from
prisons,

So fairy tales aren't real,
But no, they're not dead.
I became an adult when
I realized, there is glorious life–
Outside of playing pretend.

Thinking while I drive with one of my best friends to Corpus

The sky is opaque
Windmills wave
I'm not sure what air they are moving
Everything is still
My car is the only thing driving in a frozen frame

I will be okay.
The windmills couldn't shake
The stillness from the sky
I
am driving with one best friend
To see another

From love, with love, for love
I
am as firmly rooted as the sky
Small towns with dirty secrets pass me by
I
am grateful to be alive.

On the way to the Houston Zoo lights

My sadness is palpable around me
In the passenger seat of the car
A bubble so electric
My hair is standing on end
The silence is a needle
Threatening to pop it
Tears stream down my face
The loudest emotions
Are the most quiet.

Pulled out of a reverie

I'm laughing
In shades of purple
Everything is fluid all around me
I'm wide-grinned, yelling in your face
Counts—absorbed in the game
My hand shakes another's shoulder
And shakes me awake? Or asleep—
Finally
I wasn't thinking
I wasn't forcing reality
I was lost in all the motion around me
What a gift it is
To lose track—
To get lost,

You can only lose time
When you possess enough of it.

College gave me you

Leighton picks
Dead leaves off of trees
Ever so tenderly
And you know
That hers is a soul that learned to give warmth
From all of the cold she bore

Another lifetime—
You'd never know
She lived
For—Leighton lights
Underground cities
With the gold in her eyes
Leighton falls in love–
flowers begin to climb
Walls that haven't seen the light of day
In a thousand years

Leighton knows tears
So she paints sunny skies
Over everyone else's dark night

The truth is
Leighton has always been light
The spirit lit a flame behind her eyes
Before she was even born

Yes, Leighton bore the toughest winter storms
And wondered where the Others were to keep her warm
It took all the winds and all the rains
To realize she's always been the torch
And she's always had a place
At the king's table

Lights don't know they're radiating
They only see the shadows cast from their angelic faces
Do you think the sun knows how bright it is?
Yet everything aside from the sun is darkness and space.

Detour

Mirror ball

I was
Millions of tiny fragments
Mirrors cracked
By hating eyes
I
Was as broken as the sky
Thunder claps
Only
If you looked into my eyes
You saw
Sunny skies
I did my best to hide
My pieces
Cracked
I glued them back
Into a mirror ball
I reflected brilliant
Patterns
Of colored light
They tried to break me
You made me
Into wonderful
Light cast
Onto dark floors
My accusers left me crying on
And now they dance in my light—yours
Forever more.

Koinonia

Riding in the passenger seat
I am thirty minutes away from home
I am also fifty minutes away
From where I came
I am forever "there–"
Simultaneously always on the way

 That's the way life works
If you're coming, you're also going
To arrive somewhere, you depart somewhere else
You are always D
                    R
                      O
                        P
                          P
                          I
                            N
                            G

And
                                        P
                                      U

                                  G
                                N
                              I
                            K
                          C
                        I
                      P

Persevering and giving up

Right as he was slipping through my fingers
God gave something firmer to entwine my hand with
I grasped you in my palm–a solid rock
Before I even knew he was falling, he was gone
I was not
Empty handed.
Nor–
Empty hearted.
Before I could even realize I was about to lose,
I had already won.
That's what God does while you're slipping:
He provides a way
To keep you
 H o l d i n g   o n.

Persistent Rain

Nothing changed.
Except the roof that held strong through years of storms,
Finally gave way,
Not to a mighty wind—not even to a hurricane,

It finally bowed beneath
Light
Soft
Pattering rain,
That day after day,
Beat against the old stubborn roof,
Until it poured through weathered holes in the tiny house
Down into a big, blue bucket,

And that's the way healing is:
The strongest of walls—
Eventually fall, beneath
Attritious raindrops—
Relentless prayers,
That seem to bang against the tough roof, to a deaf God,

Until

Water leaks through
And gathers—
Puddles on the floor,

And there's not enough pots or pans or buckets to collect all the falling water,

Some oceans are filled, not by God unclenching his hands to release a torrent,
But drop by little drop; moment by little moment.

Unwritten

Poetry used to be the way that I healed from heartbreak
Now as soon as prose stirs in my brain
I shut it down
Cap it, pin it, throw it away
I don't even want to think of the pain,
Or of all of the ways–that I thought things would be different,
Sometimes poetry is best left unwritten.

Dear little girl,

With your smile so bright
I lost you for a while
You knew all the ways life couldn't treat you right–
Unaware –even as you smiled so wide
So genuine in pictures
Life wore on you
Like scarecrow lines
in the mirror

You saw wrinkles in the corners of your eyes
Yet you couldn't remember the last time you'd truly smiled
I look back at those times

Before

Before I realized I was being used —just happy to be needed

Before
When all I wanted was to love and didn't know it had a price

Before

Before I paid, my smile
To light another's eyes

Before I knew that two
People could light up
At the same time

When I believed that love
Required one to die
Not the way they describe at church:
A selfless kind of love–
Not that
kind of death
The death
You don't realize you die
When you're 17 and can't figure out
Why everything makes you cry
Until 22 and someone smacks you awake
You didn't realize
You'd gone to sleep for quite some time

Oh, dear little girl
You strayed so far away
I couldn't find you
Now I have
Your past can't make you
Go away

Dear little girl
Whatever you go through
You're here to stay.

Rapunzel

"Prince, save me,"
I lean out of my spiral pillar
Into a pitch black night –
All the shooting stars have died
With fairytale faith
Night after night bleeds into day after days–long–
Chestnut locks turn grey
Still locked away
Prayers fade with looming sell-by dates
Royalty expires with the hush of youthful fires
Hearses take the place of horses
Wicked witches save the day
I stay
Trapped in a tired tower
No king befitting the queen
The prince prefers beauty in spires
To adventures, true love, and breaking free
"This storybook is messed up,"
I become the moss dressing the grey cage
Sitting in my designated place
Hands folded in laps–white surrender
Then Heaven comes down to save me.

Little Things

I fell asleep to the rhythmic
Drip
      Drip
            Drip
Of a leaky faucet,

I woke up,
Went to shower,
I found
The tub, half-way filled up.

I gasped.
—astonished—
At how a steady,
Drip
      Drip
            Drip
Could collect much more water than time.

Kindness is this way,
A Drip
      Drip
            Drip
A swift hello,
A quick smile,
An extra beat of the clock taken to hold open a door.

If you feel
–Unseen–
Handing out pieces of yourself
In a self-consumed society,

Remember,
It takes drops,
To make waves,
And I'm fully convinced
That Jesus made the ocean
Exactly this way.

Don't judge a book by its cover

People are slipping
Butter between my fingers
The tighter I grip
The more liquidy-stick-
iness drips through my palms
The more I hold on
The less you look like you
From when we began.

The pitfall of being an optimist

I fell for
It
Again

A drunk text
A fake friend

A knight in shining
Armor?
No– lies.

Not everything that catches your eye—
Is *brilliant.*

Ammo that lies in wait

I go to Hotworx
My aunt died right after working out there
Brain aneurysm
My mom blames the heat
But the heat just caused the barrel to explode

For all our monument making and cave wall painting
Our species
Has always been
Flammable.

I wonder if you bought my poetry book

Dear Ex-Boyfriend,

Cheers! You made it onto printed pages!

Were you angry
When I villainized you—
Victimized you?

Aren't they the same thing?
At least—
That's what *you* taught me.

You won't make the news like you always wanted
But you're still splashing the headlines of my daily haunting.

#15

The loudest emotions
Are the most quiet
The grave expression
At the funeral
The blank face
In the corner
Unreadable
Some emotions are too heavy
For an open book
And classics
Are often the least read
Among the most common.

Weapons

My thoughts:
Bullets
Words
Shells flying
Stinging hot
¿How many
Do I have to say–
To put a hole in the page?

Escape

Comes in many forms
I am an explorer of uncharted worlds
Of deep and raging seas and windy skies
All the places you can go when you open your mind
All the places you can leave behind
When you open
your heart.

I'm too heavy to be a puppet

I am
A string
Held up by something
In the sky
It pulls me tight
And if it even gives
A little
I will come apart
In p i e c e s.

For the better

We say that a lot–
When calamity strikes
When we lose the ones we love

We say it
Because it's *true*–
And painful

I'm driving down a county road
The sky is full of rain
Doubt drizzles into a downpour of broken faith
I question
The validity of
"For the better"

I look up
I'm driving through a rainbow
It shines starkly against foreboding clouds
End to end
The whole arc
While the rain violently pours down

You can simultaneously drive through thunder and rainbows
Walk through the promise and the pain
We think the sun only comes out after the rain is gone
But there that rainbow was–brilliant against haunting skies and

harsh rain

At once I understood what God was saying:
"This storm *is* my deliverance from your pain."
The rainbow is the rain.

Hannah

She makes
My glass shards
Into mirror balls
Loves the broken
Right out of me
She makes
Ugly tears
Into crystal streams
She is
Constant
Unchanging
The best part of my Father's face
She is grace upon grace–
The kind of company that stays
When you can't comprehend
The human experience
And makes
It worthwhile
While you're breaking–
She is
A lily of the field–
Quiet beauty unfading.

A time to scatter stones and a time to gather stones

I collected flat stones at the lake, making a bucket with my hands,
While watching kids weigh down their shirt and jean pockets
collecting them
They must have forgotten–they only pooled all those pebbles to
scatter them–
Skip them–

You can only carry rocks in your pockets for so long–
Stones are meant to be gathered,
So they can skip on silver midnight lakes,
Paint miraculous ripples

Stones aren't meant to stay–
Making bulges of your pockets,
Burdening you with weight,

We like to trap beauty–to display it–

The most beautiful things,
Are never meant to stay–
Lodged between panes of glass,
Becoming dusty with display,

No, beauty always runs away–
Beauty is change.

It seems—
The ruddy-cheeked kids,
Stockpile stones,
Just in time for their parents to tell them it's time to leave.

We gather stones, then we scatter them,
Goodbyes are a pretty thing.

Acknowledgments

Sana Sana was my own medicinal song during a trying time. I wrote these words the way my mother sang them over my fevered head–reassuringly and pouring healing with every stroke.

I must first thank my professors Dr. Chelsey Clammer and Dr. Sonia Del Hierro who helped me see that the magic in my prose was as real as any alma de casa's song. I wouldn't have had the confidence to give flesh to bones otherwise.

Every story has a beginning–mine, was the border town, McAllen, TX. Special thanks to my parents for creating me, for having the faith to set me free into the quaint Austin suburb of Georgetown, TX. It was here in the town of flourishing poppies that I realized the tattered fragments of leather on my back were actually wings. Thanks for helping me fly, for praying at every pit stop, and pointing my head to the sky each time I was faced with confusion that threatened to ground me.

Thank you to Leighton Dorman, a fellow kindred soul I found at Southwestern University. You've had a hand in this book from the beginning. You've edited my drafts on stressful mornings, sharpened my ideas, and most of all, simply done life with me, and in doing so, inspired my pen.

I thank my soul sisters Hannah Rodriguez and Danielle Renaud. In kindergarten, teachers likened empathy to climbing in the pit with the wounded soul rather than standing above it and watching.

That's exactly what you both have done the past four years of my life. When it rained, you walked alongside me with an umbrella. When it froze, you gave me handheld warmers and bore the cold beside me. Every time the sun shines, you put on your sundress and dance with me. You created space for me to cry, dance, mourn, and heal. For that, I am eternally grateful and hope to keep stomping in the rain with you forever.

Lastly, thank you to Avery Castillo, Edward Vidaurre, and every member of FlowerSong Press for bringing my dreams to life and continually holding space for the voices of those who otherwise might be drowned out.

Author Bio

Ashlynn Delias was homegrown in McAllen–a south Texas town on the Mexican border. She studied English and religion at Southwestern University where she further fell in love with the written word. When she isn't perusing poetry at the local bookshop, she's selecting the next dark read for her book club. She draws inspiration from her mixed Mexican roots and her love of the Victorian era. She's a writer to the core and a reader far deeper, but most of all a fellow pioneer traipsing life's wilderness. Ashlynn is a firm believer that all things beautiful ache–poetry, music, film, and life. Keep up with her next journey through her socials:

IG: @scrawledinashes
TikTok: @scrawledinashes

FLOWERSONG
PRESS

**FlowerSong Press nurtures essential verse
from, about, and throughout the borderlands.
Literary. Lyrical. Boundless.**

Sign up for announcements about
new and upcoming titles at:

www.flowersongpress.com

www.ingramcontent.com/pod-product-compliance
Lightning Source LLC
Chambersburg PA
CBHW030457130626
46549CB00007B/2763